W9-AYZ-271

Words of Welcome

Words of Welcome
. . . and More Ideas
for Speakers and Writers

Amy Bolding

Baker Books

A Division of Baker Book House Co
Grand Rapids, Michigan 49516

© 1965 by Baker Book House

Published by Baker Books
a division of Baker Book House Company
P.O. Box 6287, Grand Rapids, MI 49516-6287

Previously published under the title *Words of Welcome: And Other Helps for Speakers*

New paperback edition published 2001

Printed in the United States of America

Library of Congress Cataloging-in-Publication Data

Bolding, Amy
    Words of welcome : —and more ideas for speakers and writers / Amy Bolding.
    Originally published: Grand Rapids, Mich. : Baker Book House, 1965.
    ISBN 0-8010-6398-1 (paper)
    1. Speeches, addresses, etc. I. Title. II. Series.

PN6122 .B65   2001
815´.54—dc21   2001043223

Scripture is taken from the King James Version of the Bible.

For current information about all releases from Baker Book House, visit our web site:

                http://www.bakerbooks.com

Contents

Preface

So you have been asked to make an introduction, give a word of welcome, or just plain make a speech! You are thrilled at the honor. You are excited over the chance to give your opinion. But there are some things to remember if you really want to go over with your audience.

A very important thing is to have something to say. Know what you plan to say and be sure you are saying what you want people to hear. The way to accomplish this is to write out your message, no matter how long or short. After it is written, read it aloud to yourself and see if it sounds the way you expected it to.

After your message is prepared and you have confidence that it will go over with a bang, think of some other ways of pleasing an audience.

Look your best. Many people have gotten jobs over others because they polished their shoes brighter and pressed their clothes to sharper creases. I have often heard the motto repeated: "A man's success depends upon his looking his best."

Remember when you look your best you have more confidence in yourself. Always stand or sit erect.

You are selling something to your audience. Be a good salesperson. Make them like you, and your product or the person you are introducing goes over better.

A good salesperson always smiles. Don't sit on the stage with a sad look—smile!

A joke in good taste will catch people's attention. People will listen better after you have their attention.

When you reach the climax, don't drag on and on like molasses stringing from a spoon on a cold morning. Speak your piece and shut up!

You may not be a cultured lady or gentleman, but there may be some in your audience, so act like one. Let what you say be appropriate for the occasion.

Remember when introducing someone, you are not the main speaker; leave him or her a little time.

Above all, try to believe what you are saying. Say it with the most pleasing voice possible. Even if your knees are playing a knocking song, act poised. Never look constantly at the ceiling. Your audience wants to see your eyes as you talk. Do not be afraid to use a little imagination and make what you are saying live.

> Just to make this book exciting,
> And make your life worthwhile,
> Always start your message
> With a great big SMILE.

Introductions

For Men

Our speaker today is one who has with patience and per-
severance tried to be an instrument of peace in the world.
Through the fleeting years of life, he has devoted much
time to travel and speaking in the interest of a better
nation and a better world. He has brought comfort and
courage to many hearts.

When he comes to the end of the way, I am sure he
will hear the King of kings say: "Well done, thou good
and faithful servant. . . . enter into the joy of thy Lord"
(Matthew 25:23).

With great honor I present Mr. _____ to you.

Today I want to introduce to you a man whose heart
and soul are filled with the love of God. He yearns to
share that love with all men. He reaches far, enriching
the lives of all he touches. As you listen, I think your

own heart will be touched with his love and zeal for kingdom work.

It is hard to keep God-centered in the hurry of this rushing modern world, but as you listen to our speaker today, you will say: "It is good to be here."

Mr. _____, we welcome you with all our hearts.

Someone has said that the marks handed out in the school of experience are black and blue. Mr. _____, our speaker for the hour, has certainly had much experience in his field of service. I am sure we will listen with interest as he tells us of some of those marks handed to him in this school of experience.

It is with great pride that we present, for your enjoyment and pleasure, the one who comes to speak this evening. He will bring to us a thoughtful presentation of inspiration and devotion.

I present to you a man who speaks with homey philosophy. He is filled with true neighborliness. He is an inspiration to our Christian world. The more honors and prizes he wins, the more humble and grateful he grows.

As graduates you are about to embark into the exciting world of making your own way. Our speaker is old enough to know the problems you will face; he is young enough to remember when he too was a graduate.

I want to introduce to you one you rely on, one you respect, one you depend on, one you appreciate, one you trust, one you know and love—our pastor.

We do not need a prophet to tell us these are troubled times in which we live. All avenues of life are affected by them. Times as these drive those who fear God to their knees. In the face of growing unconcern for morals and better living standards, our speaker tonight has waged a battle to make our world better.

He has gone up and down our state, preaching and teaching a better way. He has written articles and books on the subject of moral decline. We are glad to see so many of our young people here tonight. Our speaker has a message of encouragement for you.

Our young people are still challenging us with the sincere work they are doing. They seem to have boundless energy and unlimited faith. It is a pleasure to introduce to you a young man as our speaker.

Well, I am glad to say he is a little older than he was a few years ago. When he was in kindergarten, he rushed home one day and excitedly made a request of his mother.

"Mommy, I have to have a gun belt with some holsters and guns."

"What on earth for, Son?" she asked him.

"Teacher said tomorrow she's going to teach us to draw."

I hear he is still good on the draw. I am sure he will hit the bull's-eye as he speaks to us today.

Since Homecoming Week has such far-reaching influence, we appointed a committee to select our speaker for the day. After careful consideration, the committee chose one whom we are proud to call a graduate of our school.

We cordially welcome him back to our campus today. We shall continue to rejoice in the things Mr. _____ has accomplished since his graduation.

We have been again and again impressed with the remarkable progress of our speaker's organization. He has worked at starting new methods of procedure.

We gratefully call attention to the fact Mr. _____ has traveled quite a distance in order to speak to us today. Since his time is very valuable, we feel he paid us a great compliment by consenting to come.

I come to introduce to you today a man who puts spiritual things first in his life. We endorse Mr. _____ and the work he represents. He is a man of exceptional ability and training. He is also a native of our section of the country. He understands our problems and our way of life. He renders valuable service as he goes about so willingly and tells his experiences.

No man among us has meant more to our denomination. He is a Spirit-filled, Christlike leader.

It is not an easy task to try to crowd a year's report into one brief message, as we are asking our speaker to do today. He will not have time to tell us all that has been accomplished in his field of service. We can only hope he will stir us to such an extent that we will pray for him and back him more fully as he goes back to his field of work.

Every contact I have had with this man who comes to speak today has been one of inspiration and blessing. I only wish all of you could know him better. His devotion and loyalty to Christ, his untiring and self-sacrificing service, have been an example to all who know him. I consider it a wonderful opportunity just to be able to say a few words of introduction for one who gives of himself so freely for the Master's use.

For more than twenty-five years, Mr. _____ has served churches in our area. He is held in highest esteem all over our state. He is ever mindful of the task that claims priority in a minister's life. I praise God for this modest, unassuming servant.

We will hear gladly our fellow worker and brother in Christ.

✐

Mr. _____ has a vigorous personality. He serves as pastor in the heart of a growing city. He is a well known and deeply appreciated figure in our denomination. It is with great pleasure I present to you Mr. _____.

✐

We feel honored tonight to have Mr. _____ as our guest speaker. He has had much experience with counseling people. I feel sure he will help you work out the puzzle of some of life's problems.

Mr. _____ is very much in demand as a speaker, and we are fortunate indeed to have the pleasure of hearing him speak tonight.

Mr. _____, we will listen gladly to your words of wisdom.

✐

In looking about for a commanding personality to lead us in our study concerning the perplexities of today's problems, we sought one able to speak with persuasive authority. Mr. _____ is just such a man. He has made extensive studies of our world problems as well as local problems. He lives in our midst, and we all admire him greatly. Mr. _____, we consider it an honor to have a man of your talents as a fellow citizen. We are glad to hear you at this time.

✐

It is a great pleasure for me to introduce our speaker for the hour. Every contact I have had with this man has been one of inspiration and blessing. Mr. _____, we are honored to have you with us today. Your untiring and self-sacrificing service to the cause you represent has been an example to all of us. I consider it a wonderful opportunity just to say a few words of introduction concerning one who serves so well. Welcome, Mr. _____.

⚬

All my life I have heard of people who pulled themselves up by their bootstraps. I understand that would be an almost impossible feat. Our guest speaker tonight comes as near pulling himself up by his bootstraps as any person I know.

He recently won a great honor for his work. We are very proud of his accomplishments in his chosen field of endeavor. Long after the prize he received has been lost and forgotten, the good he accomplished will live on. Welcome, Mr. _____.

⚬

I hear Mr. _____ is a great golfer. He plays in the seventies. If the temperature gets lower than 70 degrees he just doesn't go out. We are glad he feels differently about speaking. This is a cold night, but our hearts will be warmed as we listen to his message. He has a reputation for inspiring people to go out and accomplish things for the Lord.

⚬

Our speaker today is respected and loved by all who come within the range of his leadership.

⚬

Our guest speaker is a favorite of young people. He has been named outstanding minister of the year a number of times. He is very effective as a minister. He is author of a number of books. He was awarded the Doctor of Divinity degree in _____ by _____ College.

For Women

Ms. _____ was reared in _____, where her father was a teacher in the college. She has a degree from _____ University, and she chose to be a _____. We are happy to say that her record is quite outstanding.

⚬

Henry Wadsworth Longfellow wrote as follows:

> Lives of great men all remind us
> We can make our lives sublime
> And departing leave behind us
> Footprints on the sands of time.

Tonight we have a lady to speak to us who will certainly leave behind her some wonderful footprints. She has spent her time and effort and money for many years improving conditions around her. She has brought sunshine and hope to those whose paths crossed hers.

The way to transform this world into a happy and desirable place to live is to strive to make your own corner of life better. The one I am about to introduce to you is well known for her contribution to our city as a civic leader. As we drive about our city, we can see many pleasant things she has been influential in pushing forward as civic projects. She goes about her work in such a selfless way that many people do not realize how much we really are indebted to her. I consider it a great honor to be the one to introduce Mrs. _____.

Someone a long time ago said, "Actions speak louder than words." Our speaker for this hour is one who carries a message of good news wherever she goes. She truly is a "living epistle, known and read of all men."

> Nobody's ever added up
>   The value of a smile;
> We know how much a dollar's worth,
>   The feet that make a mile;
> We know the distance to the sun,
>   The size and shape of the earth;
> But none can tell just how much
>   A happy smile is worth.

—Selected

The one I am about to introduce to you is known by all her friends for her sweet, happy smile. I can be walking along in a deep-blue mood and meet her, and just seeing her smile always gets me away from the blue mood to a pleasant one. She is known not for her smile alone, but for the fact that her life lives up to that smile.

She is uncomplaining and cheerful, spreading sunshine along the way.

We are honored to have one sing for us who is sought after by all the organizations in our city. She truly has the voice of a nightingale. We are indeed fortunate that she makes her home in _____ and is so willing to entertain with her lovely voice.

Like Esther of old, our speaker is a very beautiful and lovely lady. Like Esther, she spends much time and effort in behalf of her people. She is constantly striving to obtain better living conditions and better educational advantages for those she calls her own people.

"Ten men banded together in love, can do what ten thousand separately would fail in," wrote Carlyle.

Mrs. _____ has banded many more than ten women together for the cause of missions. We are happy to say that we are really making great strides for good in the mission phase of our denomination. We will hear her prayerfully as she tells us about our mission projects.

Guess what we've got at our house.
    A baby that's brand new,
He has a tiny dimple, and eyes of the deepest blue,
    His mouth is like a rosebud—
But there's no teeth inside.
    I know it for I peeped to see,

Last evening when he cried.
   His ears are just like sea shells
So tiny and so flat, but, say,
   He has no hair at all
To rumple with his hat.
   I wonder why dad bought him
Before he was all done—
   But mother says when he grows big
We'll both have lots of fun!

                    —Anonymous

Now I know some of you are thinking, "How did he find such a lovely woman to be our speaker?" Well, I guess you will have to be like the little girl with the new baby brother. Wait and see how much fun we have listening to this pretty young miss. You see, I am her baby brother, and we really have had fun!

Mrs. _____ is a woman of wit and wise charm. She is a delightful discovery as a speaker. She blends graceful and good-humored satire with moments of the most serious thoughts on problems of today.

You will find Mrs. _____ to be unusually appealing when she talks about the cause she works so hard to help.

We are honored to have Mrs. _____ as our guest tonight.

The talented Mrs. _____ lists her present occupation as "wife and mother," but she is a very busy person in many other ways. She often serves in a voluntary capacity at the local hospital. She is also on several committees for local civic projects. Mrs. _____, we are so glad you took time from your very busy schedule to be our speaker tonight.

Our guest at this time is a very important person in the organization she represents. She is very sweet and generous to spend some time with us. It is nice to be important, but it is also important to be nice. I introduce to you one who is both important and nice.

We all admire people who have some objectives in life. Our speaker for today is one who has a glorified objective. In order to accomplish such an objective, she is giving much of her time and talents to telling others. Mrs. _____, we are glad to hear you at this time.

In the heart of almost all of us there smolders a desire to get close to Mother Nature. We often paint pictures in our minds of the home we yearn for in the country. Most of these dreams are vague and uncertain. Today we have as our guest one who has gotten close to Mother Nature in her own backyard. Mrs. _____ has won a number of prizes with her beautiful flowers. Her home is a showplace for flower lovers. We hope she will tell us some of her secrets and inspire us to grow more and better flowers.

∽

Miss _____, we are glad you could be with us today. Your reputation for lifting people up to higher planes of thinking has long been known by most of our group. You seem to have found the secret of the true thinker. Your articles are always read with interest, and we feel you accomplish great good with your writing.

You are a guest we have anticipated for some time, and we welcome you most heartily.

∽

Having known _____ several years ago as a student leader and a promising scholar, I was not surprised when I read of her most recent success as an artist. She is such a courageous young woman who has always refused to be a quitter. I am proud to introduce to you an old friend and one I admire greatly.

For Doctors

We are so honored tonight to have Dr. _____ speak to us. Early in life he dedicated himself to the study of medicine. He spent long, hard years of study and work to reach the position he now holds in the medical profession. More than a few owe their lives to him and his skill as a doctor.

He is so kind to come here to speak when his time is so taken up with healing the sick. He serves on some hospital boards and is active in civic affairs in our city.

Dr. _____, we feel greatly honored to have you for our guest speaker today.

⁓

Almost all my memories of Dr. _____ are bound up in our life together as schoolboys. From him I learned that devotion to one's task can transform drudgeries into joy and delight. From him I learned one could have fun and still take time to study and learn at school.

Dr. _____ has made a large contribution to the school where he has spent many years as a professor. He has influenced many young people to live up to the best of their abilities.

I present to you our distinguished speaker of the hour, Dr. _____.

⁓

The average layperson has only a fair conception of the ramifications in the activities of a hospital. Dr. _____ is going to bring to our minds the broad scope of the institutions of healing.

⁓

Dr. _____ is a faithful and most highly valued member of our organization. She has always been ready to respond when called upon, regardless of her very busy schedule. Her contributions in time and money have promoted the interests of our cause.

I consider it a great honor to be able to introduce Dr. _____ to you. He is a greatly useful and distinguished Christian citizen.

Most of those present today have trusted their lives to the Great Physician, our Lord and Savior, Jesus Christ. There is one here to speak to us today who has gone near and far healing the sick. She too has trusted her life to the Great Physician. Because she does love God she spends part of her time telling the story of her life and conversion.

We are so glad to have so dedicated a person of medicine to speak at this time.

Our guest speaker for the evening is a favorite of young people. He is Dr. _____, who has been named outstanding Doctor of the Year by the local Medical Society. He is famous in our state for the success he has achieved as a surgeon. He devotes some time to the clinic for underprivileged children each week.

I remember Dr. _____ from our boyhood together. I have memories of many boyish pranks we enjoyed together. Perhaps it would be best for me not to tell any boyhood stories. I present to you our distinguished speaker for the hour. Dr. _____, we are honored to have you.

We have been told that moral disease is incurable by human power. It bids defiance to medical skill, and resists all human effort.

Dr. _____, our guest tonight, is a medical doctor. She is very busy in the hospital where she is employed, yet she very often spends her evenings going out speaking, seeking to make our world a better place morally as well as physically.

God has provided a remedy for moral disease. Yet he needs a moral agent to tell of the cure. Dr. _____ very unselfishly gives of her time to be just such an agent. We welcome such a great doctor as our guest.

Reading in a medical magazine the other day, I discovered people spend the most money on seeking relief from ailments which do not exist. To say the least, this is not a healthy situation.

We have invited Dr. _____ here to speak to us about ailments which do not exist. We feel grateful he has taken the time from his busy schedule to spend this hour with us.

In talking with Dr. _____ before our meeting, she told me some startling things. One of the saddest to me was the fact that many people with serious diseases could have been cured if they had visited their physician when the symptoms first started.

Dr. _____ is the type of person who keeps up with the very latest techniques and trends. We are fortunate indeed to have her speak to us.

Here we are tonight with a very eminent man to speak for us. Someone has very aptly said, "It's not what you eat that causes ulcers; it's what's eating you."

He is just the man to tell us how to get rid of the things which worry us.

Tonight we have with us a distinguished surgeon from a distant city. Dr. _____ has had some trying and some funny experiences as he has from time to time gone to speak in strange places. Not long ago he started for a strange place for the graduation exercise of the nurses. When he was comfortably seated in the plane, he began to suffer from hayfever. His nose started running, and his nose and eyes were both pouring hot water. When he finally arrived at the hotel, he stopped and asked a boy the directions to the hospital.

"Now, please mister, don't cry so," the little boy told him. "If you have to go to a hospital and be operated on, they will chloroform you first."

The good Doctor wiped away the hayfever tears and started for the hospital, muttering, "If there is any putting to sleep to be done, I'll do it with my speech."

Dr. _____ has learned to be an optimist. The other night he was called out into the dark by a pleading voice.

He arrived to find one of those places where the rats are so thick they lick the cat. The roof leaked and the children looked hungry. It was just that kind of place. The poor sick mother said to her doctor, "Isn't it lucky that when it rains the roof leaks over the bathtub?" This brave man will now address us.

Dr. _____, our speaker for the evening, is free from dictation from any group or organization. She feels called of God to give a testimony of her Christian experiences. She speaks fearlessly. She is a world spirit. She loves all men and races.

As I introduce our guest, please allow me to pay tribute to my most worthy predecessor. All I have learned about her is commendable.

For Teachers

For our speaker today we have a man to whom students instinctively respond. His leadership in student activities on his own campus is quite outstanding. Only time and eternity will reveal the good this man has accomplished as he works with boys and girls. I am proud to have a child enrolled in the school he represents.

Our speaker this evening stands tall, not only physically, but as an educator. He is known as an outstanding teacher. When he speaks, he presents the truth of our educational system with clarity and perception.

I predict you will go away tonight with renewed interest in our educational system and those who make it work. Professor _____, we count it an honor to have you as our guest this evening.

Ms. _____ is a teacher of outstanding ability. She speaks with a simplicity of words we can understand. Her thoughts concerning modern-day education are fresh and clear-cut. She has been uncompromising in her efforts to make our schools the best in the state.

Let us concentrate on her deep, probing message concerning our complacency toward our schools.

Our speaker for this evening has a unique motto. Unlike so many schoolteachers, he does seek to find the good and the best in the young people he teaches. For his life's motto he has used the thought: "The common young people can fill a mission in life, the same as the loud and great."

I believe after hearing him speak, you will go out with renewed determination to fill your mission in life.

❧

Dr. _____ has made a place for himself in our city. We always look forward to hearing him speak. He is not quite so important in the eyes of his maid. Last week, the family was away from home when the phone rang. The maid answered.

"Is this Dr. _____'s home?" a distressed voice asked.

"Oh, yes, this is their home," the maid replied.

"Could I speak to the doctor? I need one right away, and we are strangers in town."

"Well, he isn't here, and besides, if he was, he is not the kind of a doctor that is good for doctoring folks," the helpful maid told her caller.

Now we feel Dr. _____ will be good for doctoring our thoughts and minds tonight.

❧

Dr. _____ has spent many years teaching in our public schools. She is a graduate of _____ and has a Ph.D. from _____. She has traveled extensively in the United States and abroad. We consider it a great honor for her to spend an evening telling us some of the things she has observed during her many years as a teacher.

❧

Mr. _____ is known for his unswerving loyalty to the best interest of his pupils. His radiant smile and gentle voice, his encouragement in times of struggle are stamped on the memory of his pupils. I always like to meet Mr. _____ on the street and feel the clasp of his cordial handshake.

He has served our city schools well. We are fortunate to have him as our speaker this evening.

It is a pleasure to introduce to you Dr. _____, who is head of our own Christian school. The future of our denomination leadership depends upon our school being strong. Our dear leader strives to train our young people in body, mind, and soul. Dr. _____ has maintained a good curriculum without sacrificing the cultural and Christian atmosphere of the school.

Ms. _____, it gives me great pleasure to introduce you to the people in my hometown tonight. Ms. _____ is a college graduate and former schoolteacher. Driven by a desire to do more and improve moral conditions in some sections of our large cities, she has devoted all her time for the past several years as a social worker.

She is a woman who is helping history be made. I am glad we have this opportunity to hear more about her work and how we may be able to help with it.

Dr. _____ was my teacher in college, and so I am doubly proud to be asked to introduce him tonight. As students we knew him as a very dedicated man. He expected us to do our best work and was willing to help us over the rough spots.

He comes to grips with the problems of everyday living. He offers a plan for dealing with them.

At times as a college boy, I thought he was too strict, too demanding. Now I wonder why he didn't make us work harder. Dr. _____, we welcome you tonight as a dear friend and a great educator.

Professor _____, we are so glad to have you with us as our guest. You are a person who strides into each day and each new experience with joy and confidence. As students we always enjoyed your abundant illustrations from life.

If you want to be considered perfect, a possessor of all knowledge, just teach first or second grade. If you want to be considered hard-hearted and mean, just teach math and give a lot of homework. If you want to be talked about, be a coach and fail to win ball games.

Our speaker tonight is a fine teacher and fits none of these categories I mentioned. He is a science teacher. We perhaps would not understand if he talked about the subject he teaches, but we do understand some of the things he will discuss concerning everyday problems.

Professor _____, we are glad to have you speak to us.

Someone has said there are so many things to worry about nowadays that we should take the time to pick out something that really matters. We are not here to spend time worrying but listening to a very great educator speak. She has picked a subject of vital interest to each of us. A subject that really matters. There will be much in her message to help us live more fully. She presents a mature and effective philosophy of life.

Dr. _____, after your message tonight I feel we will all go forth with a new purpose in our hearts to live more victoriously day by day.

I am honored to present Dr. _____ at this time.

For Public Officials

Senator _____, we feel honored you could spare the time to attend our meeting. Some people drift along with their minds in neutral, being pushed by the strongest popular opinions of the day. Senator _____ is not that type of person. He studies the issues of our day and tries to the best of his knowledge to make wise decisions.

Senator _____ is a popular man in our section of the state. We feel he has a noble purpose in his heart. He considers the good of the ones who helped put him in office. Senator, as long as you continue to serve our interest so well, you may be assured of our support. Welcome!

It is a pleasure for me to present our honorable mayor tonight. We have been friends for some time. I have found her to be a person who plans ahead. At times she has had disappointments, but these only make her more determined to renew her efforts to make ours an outstanding city. She is a good leader and we are proud of our mayor.

∽

Van Wyck Brooks wrote: "Without leaders, we cannot have a great society."

The public servant I introduce to you tonight is the type of person who many times defers his personal advancement to the ambitions of others. We have found from past records that he is an effectual leader. He hopes for an improvement in our society and times.

Mr. _____, we will gladly hear what you have to tell us of our present situation.

∽

Someone has called our speaker of the hour an average American young person. I would never assume to judge what comprises the so-called average American. But I do wish to say that our honored guest is a very fine young politician. It would be well for our country and state if more young people of her ability and training entered the political field.

There is much at stake in our world today. Ms. _____, we are proud to have you hold a public office in our county.

∽

Our city is experiencing good and prosperous times. We are proud of our city officials. Mr. _____ is one we are especially glad to call our friend. He seeks to help us have an increased awareness of all phases of our city life. He seeks to communicate with the ordinary citizen by speaking to our different organizations and explaining the workings of our city government. Mr. _____, we hear you gladly.

ॐ

We feel the magnitude of the presence of our speaker. She is noted for her wit, so be prepared for an evening of fun as well as serious thoughts. Ms. _____ is one of our most respected public officials. It is our good fortune that she was born in our state and is devoting her life to serving us.

We are proud of the fine tradition connected with her name. She has scholastic achievements which make her capable of holding her own with the most gifted of lawmakers. Ms. _____, we are eagerly awaiting your message.

ॐ

Senator _____ is known for his great political insight and his human compassion. Senator, your perceptive reports on world affairs give us renewed courage and hope. Senator _____ is popular for his homegrown version of politics. Being common people, we can understand his talks. Senator, we are looking forward to a great hour together.

ॐ

Many people are indignantly critical of our public officials. We need to learn lessons from history. There are those in all walks of life who deserve some criticism; on the other hand, there are those in all walks of life who serve with quiet dignity in an honest and unselfish way.

The one who speaks to us tonight has won the respect and affection of all who know her. She feels now is the time to take a stand for good government and she is taking that stand. We are indeed honored to have Governor _____ in our city tonight and as our guest speaker.

Mr. _____, we are so glad to have you with us on this occasion. We thank you so much for the help and advice you have given our people as our city has undertaken this project. We feel you are especially nice. This is a day we will not soon forget. There can be no growth without struggle. Under the leadership of our able officials, our city has grown and matured. Today, we feel a sense of achievement. Mr. _____, with many thanks for your part in our city's growth, we welcome you as you speak at this time.

Robert Louis Stevenson said: "To travel hopefully is a better thing than to arrive, and true success is to labour."

Under the leadership of Ms. _____ we have traveled hopefully toward the goal of a better state. We feel that many fine and wonderful improvements have been made. It is a joy to have you with us today. We will hear you with hope for better things to come.

Our speaker is known for his pleasant smile. He has a purpose in life, his purpose being to make our country a better place to live. He has served long and well as a public official. Oh, yes, I was going to tell you the secret of his pleasant smile, often in the face of opposition. For a motto he uses: "Keep the sunshine ever before you, and the shadows will fall behind."

Mr. _____, we are proud of the accomplishments you have been responsible for in our country. We are glad for this opportunity to hear your future plans.

∽

It is valuable when looking for a job to have both education and experience. Our speaker is just such a person. She worked her way through college. She told me she has no idea what taught her the most, the job or the school. At any rate, she could say she had experience and also a degree when she was finished. For so young a person, she has found great favor with the voters of our community. We feel she is well qualified for the place we have given her in our city government. We feel she is already working to make our town a better place to do business, to live, and to rear children.

Ms. _____, we are all interested in our hometown, so we are interested in what you have to tell us about your plans for our city's growth.

For Prizewinners

We have known _____ as a hardworking fellow student. He is always ready to help those who might be falling behind and say a cheerful word to one who seems blue or discouraged. To use a timeworn expression, he is "the salt of the earth."

Because he is so much one of us and yet so outstanding in many ways, it gives us much pleasure and satisfaction to present to _____ today the award for achievement.

∽

Ms. _____ is a member of a pioneer family in our county. She has been quite unselfish in her work for community betterment. So it is with a great deal of satisfaction we present to her this award.

∽

You have often heard it said: "If you want something done, call on a busy person."

That is just what we did. When we decided our club would enter this contest, we picked the busiest person in the club to represent us. We were not surprised when _____ won the prize. _____ has been a constant source of inspiration for all of us. We are very honored today to present the trophy to _____.

∽

There is a challenge facing us now. We have a prizewinner in our midst. We will want to make him welcome on our campus this week. I know you will continue to do a good job, as always, in taking care of visitors.

The honoree I am speaking of is our distinguished Mr. _____, a winner of prizes all over our state for _____.

∽

We are proud of the accomplishment of _____ in the athletic world. We feel honored she would take time to come and give us her testimony this morning. She is known for her fair play and good spirit of competition as well as her excellent ability to get out there and win the game.

∽

We are giving a token of our esteem and love to Mr. _____ today. For many, many years he has been one of those "last-to-leave, first-to-arrive" members. He has served us well and faithfully. He has given fullest cooperation in carrying out the projects and activities of our organization.

∽

It gives me great pleasure tonight to introduce to you one who is already a legend in her profession. She has won prizes and recognition for her outstanding ability. Her books have been published and read widely. She is really a prizewinner in the field of journalism.

Ms. _____, welcome to our meeting. We are honored you could come.

∽

Mr. _____, this pin is an award given in recognition of your loyalty and attendance during the last year. May God be praised and God be blessed as you continue in Christian loyalty and service.

∽

Our church owes a deep debt of gratitude to so many who made this building a reality by their diligent efforts over many weeks, months, and years. With the help of many people in a multitude of ways, this building has come into being.

Therefore, in sincere appreciation, may we use this plaque to help us know some who have served in this endeavor. The names on this plaque are only a few, as others served in many capacities.

For Missionaries

It is hard for me to express the deep feelings I have for our missionaries. Our speaker tonight is a missionary I admire greatly. He gave up so many things most of us think important in order to go to a foreign land and represent Christ's cause.

We will receive real blessings as we hear this man of God speak to us.

ళ్ళ

What a delightful surprise when I received a letter from _____ saying he would be in our city at this time. I rushed around making all kinds of arrangements so we could have a "real missionary" speak to us. Our guest has done so much for the Lord in his few short years in _____. We are excited and honored to have him speak today.

ళ్ళ

You do not have to cross the ocean or the continent to communicate the love of Jesus. You can go down almost any street and find someone who needs to hear the story. Our speaker at this time is _____. He told the story at home, but he could not be satisfied until he had told it to those in a foreign land. He has served _____ years in _____ and is now home for a few months' rest. I am afraid we are so eager to hear of his experiences we will let him rest very little.

ᗱ

Ms. _____ works with the refuge center in _____. Someone has said of her, "Love transforms all whom it touches." She has spent the very best years of her life for the people in her territory. She teaches Bible classes. She counsels with those who need advice. Many respond to her sincere efforts to be of service. To those underprivileged people she gives the message, "Jesus loves you and I love you."

Ms. _____, we are eager to hear some of your experiences.

ᗱ

Various missionary societies have contributed to the work of our mission speaker today. We have felt close to you as we read your letters in the mission magazines. Mr. _____, we feel you are a man who has truly given himself for service. We want you to tell us about your work. Only as we help those who go to fields away from home can we feel we too are doing mission work.

I venture the hope that after we hear your message, our offerings and efforts for missions will greatly increase.

We do not know what God will do as a result of prayer until we pray. Mr. _____ is a man who prayed for a way to serve as a missionary. God answered that prayer. We need the spiritual blessings we will receive from hearing about the marvelous work he has been accomplishing in his chosen field. He has brought a new day to mission work in _____. We are glad to hear of his work at this time.

Two of his fellow workers and Mr. _____, our guest today, went to visit an African chieftain. They hoped to gain permission to hold services at a certain place. The African dignitary looked them over and then asked a profound question.

"Are you men real or are you synthetic?"

We too have heard the word synthetic used a lot, but I can assure you our guest is very real and very worthy of our attention at this time.

Our missionary speaker today will take us into a fascinating realm of study and thought. In connection with her work she has traveled extensively. Just to hear her talk of some of the places she has been is of interest, but to hear her talk of her love for the Lord and the spread of his word is to find yourself on a higher spiritual plane. We welcome you, Ms. _____.

࿔

Mr. _____ holds a theological degree and often reads the latest theological treatises, but above all, he knows the Lord. As a young Christian with joy and purpose in his heart, he set about to win others. His wife and friends tell me he is unselfish in every way. He is making his influence felt for good.

Today, many people have a brighter look in their eyes and a happier outlook in their hearts because of the mission work done by _____ and his dedicated wife. Mr. _____, we feel humble in the presence of one who works so hard for Christ's kingdom as you do.

࿔

Ms. _____ is a missionary who works with those who have lost the way and with those who have been unfortunate. It takes a great heart of love and compassion to serve in a rescue mission. She has had outstanding success in her work. She is a quiet person but one with a spring of joy in her step as she works in her appointed place. Many have told her their troubles and gone out to face life with new hope. We are happy to have you speak at this time, Ms. _____.

࿔

Someone has said that the marks handed out in the school of experience are black and blue. Mr. _____ has had much experience in his field of service. He has had times of danger in his life and has gone fearlessly on. He has helped countless numbers of young people find a better way of life. It is a joy to have Mr. _____ to tell us some of those black-and-blue marks handed to him in the school of a missionary's life and experience.

We are fortunate indeed to have one with us tonight who is aware of world conditions. Ms. _____ is a great missionary, a great traveler, and a wonderful Christian. She has the capacity for bringing those who listen into the colorful scenes of her mission field. We cannot all travel, we cannot all be missionaries, but by listening to our guest, we can feel the refreshment and true appreciation of the scenes and experiences she shares with us.

Mr. _____ has just returned from a tour of service. He has captured the thrill and wonder of the world far away from home. As we hear him tonight, we will feel a new part in our mission work. He tells me he has been living on an island of stormy humanity. He has been able to win some people and hopes to go back as soon as possible. As a Spirit-filled leader he has truly gone forth to tell others. Mr. _____, we are honored to have you represent us in _____.

Replies
to Introductions

I am afraid Mr. _____ should have looked closer before he leaped to invite me to speak. I am far from a silver-tongued orator, but I do have something on my heart, a message I hope you will receive a blessing from hearing.

ॐ

How can I hope to live up to Ms. _____'s very kind introduction? She has been my friend and co-worker for a number of years. I count it a great honor to be asked to speak in her church.

ॐ

It gives me great joy to return again to the town of my boyhood. The improvements I see on every hand show me you are a progressive people. I am vitally interested in the churches and schools of your city. Like all growing boys, I wanted to get away at one time, to see the other side of the mountain, so to speak; but now I am home again for this occasion, and I feel honored and happy you asked me to be your speaker today.

It will be gratifying for you to know that I esteem the one who introduced me. Her usefulness has increased from year to year, and we recognize in her one of the truly great leaders of our denomination.

In every period of history, church history that is, there have been some outstanding men who graced the ministry. I like to think of your dear pastor as one of those. He holds up high standards to all those with whom he comes in contact.

It is a thrilling experience to have Ms. _____ introduce me. Her kind words make me feel humble and grateful for the privilege of speaking to you today.

Evidences of your kind interest in the cause I represent encourage me to believe we will have a profitable time together.

Men and women, organizations, institutions, many others I could name, are always planning some project—some trip or series of trips. Whatever we plan, it must eventually reach the climax and the end. A trip comes to an end, a life comes to an end, a day comes to an end.

Today we are meeting to commemorate the end of your very successful campaign for funds to be used in erecting a new building. I feel greatly honored that you asked me to speak. There are many in the audience who have worked hard and faithfully to bring about the success of this campaign. For those who will not have an opportunity to speak, I wish to say: "May God's richest blessings fall upon you for the unselfish way you have worked."

Brother _____ surely makes a nice introduction. I was wondering what he was going to say next when he just stopped. I have heard that lots of windbags are puncture-proof. Now if you believe all the kind things he said about your speaker, you might decide you have a speaker who is puncture-proof.

Sometimes one has to be puncture-proof when fighting for a cause. There will be darts hurled from every side if we dare to stand against the throng.

Thank you, Sister _____, for your kind introduction. My one qualification for attempting this work is that I feel God called me and has thus far helped me each step of the way. I want to speak to glorify my Savior. If any of you listening today put your life wholly in the hands of God, you will find great joy and perhaps many hardships.

I owe a great debt of gratitude to the one who has so graciously introduced me. From him I have learned many things. He has courage in an emergency; he is always found standing for the right. In our denomination, we have learned to look to him for leadership in answering some of today's problems.

As I stand before you today, I am realizing the fulfillment of a dream. For a number of months since your president asked me to come at this time, I have dreamed and planned for this opportunity. Your organization is outstanding in our state, and many people covet the opportunity you have given me today. We are very proud of the work accomplished by your organization.

Thank you for your kind introduction. You know this is my home state. My work has carried me elsewhere, but every time I have opportunity to come back, I wonder why I ever left. You do things in such a big and wonderful way here. I am always proud to say I am a native of this great state.

A Chinese answer to a well-deserved and thoughtful compliment is: "Flowers leave part of their fragrance in the hand that bestows them." That is the way I feel about the kind introduction.

There is one statement I never grow tired of hearing. When people say: "We're glad to have you back."

I wish to express my love for you and my gratitude for your asking me to speak again. Each time I come to this good church, I meet someone I had not known before. I am happy to see you are still growing and going for our Lord and Savior Jesus Christ.

First I would say a word of appreciation for the beautiful way this hall has been decorated. You have shown me already that you are a people dedicated to the task.

Announcing the Offering

Ain't It the Truth!

I am a nickel.
I am on speaking terms with the candy man.
I am too small to get into the movies.
I am not large enough to buy a necktie.
I am of small consideration in the purchase of gasoline.
I am not fit to be a tip; but, believe me,
When I go to church and Sunday School
I am some money.

—Selected

Again I want to express my appreciation and that of our Board of Trustees for the unselfish support we have received. Our loyal Christian friends have given most liberally to keep our institution going.

May his hand guide us into larger gifts for the advancement of his cause and kingdom work.

The plight of the world today with all that it signifies and implies reveals the stern necessity and the supreme difficulty of finding the way of universal peace and goodwill. Christianity alone can provide the underlying motive, the true working principle, that conditions the establishment and maintenance of a democratic world order in which justice and righteousness are to prevail. On this basis, we must increase our support. We must give a worthy account of our stewardship.

A needy world stands with outstretched arms. We can help. Winter is fast approaching. Millions of this earth's inhabitants will suffer and thousands will die unless you and I respond.

Time forbids me to elaborate further on the need. It is almost a colossal need. Please give without further pleading.

Our institutions are finding it quite expensive to operate during these times. We believe they are abundantly worth the cost, and in the years to come will become increasingly so.

What an investment generous donors could make by providing some of the needs of our schools.

We urge our people to make worthy and sacrificial offerings that missions around the world may be adequately supported.

We are grateful that increased financial receipts have enabled us to make improvements in the physical equipment of our plant. Yet almost countless other needs clamor for attention. Surely it is God's will for our church to enlarge our ministry. Will you match this hour of vision by making provision with your gifts?

We hear the Macedonian cry from all parts of the world. We must send people forth to tell the story of Christ. We must make other lands to "rejoice and blossom as the rose."

We must show our faith by our works and demonstrate the genuineness of our love in the proportions of our giving. We must commit ourselves to doing his will.

∽

Fall in and share the job of helping keep our work going on a cash basis.

∽

This is our urgent need. We believe you will respond in a substantial way.

∽

Remember the words of Jesus, how he said, "It is more blessed to give than to receive."

∽

Help us to recognize, O Christ, in every human need, of soul or body, your call to our hearts. Let us remember today that inasmuch as we do anything for the least of your children, we do it unto you.
Bless the gifts we bring for use in your service.
Amen.

∽

Bless thou the gifts our hands have brought:
Bless thou the work our hearts have planned.
Ours is the faith, the will, the thought;
The rest, O God, is in thy hand. Amen.

—Selected

∽

Out of thy bountiful storehouse have we all received many wonderful blessings. Now we bring our gifts to you. Use them for the extension of your kingdom in the world. Bless all who bring gifts today. In Christ's name, Amen.

Dear God, we belong to you. We bring our gifts now to your altar. Help us to be stewards for you. Make our gifts and our worship acceptable to you. Amen.

Today we think of the needs of the Church. We have many fighting the battle for good with us, but the armies of our foes are strong and bitter. We realize the harvest truly is white, but we must give generously in order to send reapers into the fields.

As we bring our gifts today, help us to remember the suffering poor, the children and youth in need of training, the people in crowded cities who need to hear your Word. May our gifts be generous and sacrificial. Amen.

For the great work of God's kingdom, we bring our gifts this morning. Dear Lord, accept them and use them for the growth of your kingdom. Send a blessing into the hearts of all who give today. Amen.

We thank you, Father, for the many blessings we have had bestowed upon us from week to week. We need your continued guidance and blessings. May our gifts today help extend the influence of our church and your cause. The gifts of those present today are gifts of love and labor. Bless the gifts in thy service and bless those who give. Amen.

We thank you for all the blessings bestowed upon us. Now with open hearts and hands, we come to bring back to you some of the provisions of your love. Lay your benediction upon our offerings. Amen.

Closing a Meeting

As we go our separate ways after the inspiration of this wonderful meeting, there comes to my mind a poem written by John Oxenham.

> To every man there openeth
> A way, and ways, and a way,
> And the high soul climbs the high way,
> And the low soul gropes the low;
> And in between, on the misty flats,
> The rest drift to and fro.
>
> But to every man there openeth
> A high way and a low
> And every man decideth
> The one his soul shall go.

As we close our meeting today, may we be strong and great in the fear of God. May we have the love of righteousness so that, being blessed of God, we may go out to become a blessing to all nations. Just for Jesus' sake.

Great men have ever been a nation's asset. Tonight we have heard one of our greatest men speak. With our world in the hands of people like this, we feel secure and unafraid.

As we go from this place tonight, may the love of God abide with us. Let us go out to be a greater blessing to all people.

For all these things we give thanks to our heavenly Father, the Giver of all good gifts. We shall return to our homes realizing that the greatest opportunities and responsibilities are before us.

We express gratitude to our heavenly Father who has blessed our efforts and to our officers and chairmen and pastors who have by their faithfulness to the task made our good reports possible.

Today we have seen how God uses individuals to promote his cause. As we go, may we commit our all to witnessing for him.

We have been on a historical pilgrimage as we listened to our guest speaker. His message has heightened our appreciation for the heritage which is ours. May we go away dedicated to future service.

Let us remember the words we have heard today and commit our substance and selves to more service in the promotion of Christ's cause around the world.

May God continue to bless you as you go out to carry forward your work in his kingdom.

The missionary messages today were so helpful and so well received by our people. Thank you for your very fine attendance today. May your lives be a blessing to all missions until Jesus comes.

May the illumination of your Spirit be round about us as we leave this sacred place. Let visions of your glory shine before us that we may find the way to serve better. May we consecrate ourselves to you and by consecration love and serve one another. Amen.

The Lord has given us today sweet messages from heaven. Let us go out as flames of fire to be instruments of service. May we long remember the great voices we have heard this day.

As we go away from this holy place, may the good seed which has been sown in our hearts bring forth abundant harvest. May we bring forth fruits of faith and obedience, through our Lord and Savior, Jesus Christ.

May all who came here today go away feeling enriched in spirit. May they have a deeper appreciation for God and his great goodness.

May we grow in grace and knowledge and in the likeness of our perfect example, Jesus Christ. Reverently we have drawn near to him. Jesus, you are our teacher. Make us wise as we live this week. Amen.

As we leave this meeting, may we determine to shape our future from the wisdom of ages past. Give us hearts of stability in this day of turmoil and conflict.

As we close this service, there is within each of us a great longing to go forth and help the bewildered world. May we always know and believe that God's power and God's might will bring ultimate victory over the puny ways of men.

As we close, let us pray for the multiplied usefulness of Christian people and for a growing spirit of evangelism and stewardship in our land. Let us pray for strong leaders who will lead us for right and righteousness. Always let us be thankful for freedom to worship as we please.

Will you sit quietly for a moment of meditation before we go? Take away the indifference to the needs of the multitudes. Have courage to go forth and speak convincingly of the wonders of his love. Amen.

May our selfish wants be lost along the way as we leave this meeting. May we be willing for God's will to be done above our own. Help us not to conform to the ways of the world in actions or attitude but to live for the highest and holiest things in life.

What a challenge we have heard today! Let us resolve to open new ways for men to hear the Word—new ways to bring people to the house of the Lord. We have heard the challenge; now comes the test of following through in our lives in the days ahead.

Let us commit our ways unto the Lord. Let us be worthy of redemption. Let us search our hearts today and ask God to use us in helping others to more abundant living.

We have seen, we have heard, we have felt the missionary message today! Will we go away and forget? Or will we go away to begin to do our part? God will go with us and give us strength for the tasks. We appreciate so very much those who have spoken and lifted us up to higher realms of missionary thoughts.

We have analyzed ourselves and faced the facts about our failures and our future. Let us determine to be Christians in all relationships.

Words of Welcome

We are happy to have you return to our city. We stand ready to help you get settled if there is anything we can do.

Our church is looking forward to you and your family attending. We cordially invite you to come and be one of us. Our church is a real "homey" church. You will find in our pastor one who understands the needs of today's families.

We surely hope to see you next Sunday.

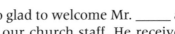

We are so glad to welcome Mr. _____ as a permanent member of our church staff. He received his Master's degree in _____. We are fortunate to secure his services. He has had several years' experience in the field of religious education. He worked part time all through school.

Mr. _____, you and your family will find we are a friendly people, and we hope to make you happy as you work for us.

Today we are privileged to welcome a new leader to our district. With the heritage of the past and the opportunity of the future, we have been looking forward to your coming, Ms. _____.

We hope you find that our district is always cooperative with your leadership. We have heard many nice things about you.

The large audience present today will show our new pastor how very much we have been looking forward to his coming.

In the short time I have known _____, I have found him to be a man of ready wit; yet his sincere love of God impresses me that he is a man who will have the ability to influence our young people.

Mr. _____, we welcome you as our new pastor and leader. We look forward to your new and stimulating thoughts and ideas.

This is a day we have awaited eagerly. Our new pastor has moved on the field and is with us for the first service as our pastor.

Our new pastor and leader is not only a good preacher but he is a person whose scholarship is at all times unimpeachable. He has a profound insight into spiritual matters. His life thus far has been a great contribution to the churches and scholars of our time.

Congratulations to our Pulpit Committee for the fine new pastor they have been able to secure. We welcome you gladly, _____. Our church has been groping along without a leader for several months. When we heard you were coming it made our whole congregation rejoice.

Your parents were members of our church in the years past. We know that from them you have received a heritage of high ideals. Checking on your career thus far, we found high ideals had marked your ministry.

We can only assure you that our church needs lots of work and encouragement. With you as our leader we look forward to a tremendous growth spiritually.

We feel honored that Dr. _____ and her family have moved to our town and especially honored that they have placed their membership with our church.

Dr. _____, we have heard so many good things about you. A doctor often has many conflicts, many calls on her time. We are so happy to have you and your family. If we can be of help or service to you in any way, be sure to consider us as your brothers and sisters in Christ and call on us.

George W. Truett, a famous Baptist minister, had a saying: "Hats off to the past! Coats off to the future!"

Our past has been fine. We are proud of a long line of pastors. Now we come to welcome a new pastor.

We must take our coats off, so to speak, and go to work helping our new leader. Dr. _____, we are very happy to welcome you.

It is an honor for me to be asked to welcome our new pastor today. I have already been to their home and met the lovely family. We shall be proud to call them "ours" during the years to come.

It is nice to be loyal to the past but now the time has arrived for us to feel it important to give devotion to our new leader. Rev. _____ comes from a good church. The people he left will feel his absence keenly: All members of our church must feel they are appointed as a committee of one to make our new pastor and family welcome.

Our sombreros are off to the committee who has so wisely selected our new leader. Ms. _____, we welcome you with open arms. Since you are from the South, we are not sure you will like our cold climate, but we wish to assure you we have a warm welcome for you and your family.

Mr. _____, we welcome you as a new teacher in our school. As you take up your new duties today, we hope you will find us helpful and friendly. We have always had a good relationship with our faculty.

Ms. _____ replaces _____, who retired last spring. You will find her an ardent fan of _____ University, the school from which she received her degree. We welcome you and hope you will be happy working here.

Ms. _____ replaces _____, who retired last spring. You will find her an ardent fan of _____ University, the school from which she received her degree. We welcome you and hope you will be happy working here.

We take this opportunity to welcome Rev. _____ to our city and to our church. He will be carrying on the city mission program for our denomination. He will inaugurate a program of service to broken homes and juvenile delinquents. He has had success in this work before moving to our city. He is an aggressive leader with a forward look.

Rev. _____ and his wife have _____ children. They will be an asset to our city, and it is with joy we welcome them into our church fellowship.

We have reason to be justly proud today. We are about to welcome in our midst a new worker with elementary children. She has been well trained in this work, and our church feels fortunate indeed to be able to secure her services. We know she will make a notable contribution to our Sunday school teaching staff.

Words of Farewell

Today we say good-bye to Ms. _____. As this young woman leaves us to go out to the mission field, I am reminded of the word CHRISTIAN.

C—onsecrated
H—umble
R—ich in fruits of the Spirit
I—nterested in people
S—low to take offense
T—actful
I—ntensely missionary
A—ble to assume responsibility
N—ot afraid of work

Can you think of anyone who fits this word more fully than _____? She will indeed be missed in our church.

◦∽◦

We regret to announce the resignation of Ms. _____. She was always busy making things go for our school. We will certainly miss her smiling face and cheerful ways.

∽

It is with tears of sadness we say farewell to our beloved pastor. He has served our church well and faithfully. He has worked hard to lay strong foundation stones for the next generation. We will pledge to him our prayers in his new field of service. We know he will not cease to pray for us in our search for a new leader. Dr. _____, we will always love you and be thankful you were our pastor for these past years.

∽

The one who leaves us today reminds me of a sign I saw in a Boston subway.

> When evening comes and shadows fall
>   And darkness hovers over all;
> When dimmed out dreary hours begin,
>   Thank God, we've still the Light within.

Although he is going far from our city, we will still remember the light of his stay with us.

∽

Some years ago a man came to live and work in our town. He made very little noise, but he was always to be found where there was sorrow or need. Today we say good-bye to this dear friend. He has felt a call to other fields of service. Although he may be away physically, he will be with us for a long time in many ways. So long as those he has helped live, they will remember and feel his presence.

✍

We wish to say farewell today to a man who has been a leader for our boys. He has promoted a program which helps keep boys healthy and happy. He has trained them in wood lore and in many survival tactics in the woods. But most important of all, by his example and word, he has taught them to walk in the ways of the Lord.

✍

There seems always to come times of saying good-bye. It falls to my lot to speak words of farewell to one of the nicest people I have ever known. For making others happy she has a way all her own. We have only the warmest feelings for Ms. _____ as she leaves us.

We will miss her cheery greetings which always seemed to come from the bottom of her heart. We can only say we envy the place to which she is moving and hope they will receive the great blessing from Ms. _____'s services which we have enjoyed.

✍

For a long time to come we will remember Ms. _____, who has worked so well with our young people. She used unusual tactics, but she always succeeded with a job well done. We wish her every joy and success in her new place of service. Her happy smile will long be remembered around here.

✍

As pastor I see many people who loudly criticize the church and its leaders. But today I am going to say farewell for all of us to one who has gone about quietly encouraging the teachers and leaders in our church. She took every opportunity to visit those in pain or in need. To me she was a "genuine" Christian.

We are sorry to lose her and her lovely family from our fellowship. I do not know an area in our church life where her influence has not been felt.

❦

Mr. _____ has given _____ years of service to our church. I want to take this opportunity to say we will miss him greatly. He has always given good service for the kingdom.

❦

It seems that our whole nation is on the move in the springtime. I just wish we did not have to see a fine couple move away from us. Mr. and Mrs. _____ have been with us while he was on sabbatical leave from his teaching position. He has spoken often to different groups in our church. He has taught us the sheer wonders of the world about us. He has inspired us to search for God's beauties of nature. We are so glad you both came our way and will always remember you with joy.

❦

In Isaiah 43:28 the chief priests were called the princes of the sanctuary. The term is often applied to the men of princely excellency and worth. As we say farewell today to one who has led us so well, surely the term "prince" would appropriately fit his character, his qualities of life and soul. He has been referred to as a denominational leader, as an executive statesman; but I believe the term "prince" would appropriately serve as being descriptive of his life.

We wish him well in his new work and home. Their gain is indeed our loss.

It is with profound regret that we announce the resignation of one who has served us well for a number of years. Perhaps we called on her too often, but she was always so gracious to speak or serve in any capacity. We will miss her so very much. She has given encouragement and guidance to many of us. We can only wish her every blessing and success in her new field of service.

We regret that it has fallen to our lot to say farewell to _____. She taught us many things during her stay among us. One of her basic philosophies was "Accept yourself." She knew her strengths and she knew her weaknesses. She faced life knowing herself. She accepted us with all our faults and our mistakes and taught us to laugh and try again. Ms. _____ knew how to make the most of every day. She never stood about waiting for real life to start. She made every project, every day, seem important.

We will miss you so very much _____, but we hope for you all the joy and happiness you have brought us.

We come today to say farewell to our pastor, who is retiring. Oh, how he has endeared himself to us during the years he spent as our pastor. He feels he has reached the age where he must pass the work to others. We have only to look about us at the many changes and improvements which have taken place during his labor among us to know how hard he has worked.

We will miss you, but we are happy for you to have time now to relax a little. Please always remember us in your prayers. We love you and hope you will return to us often.

We say good-bye to one who has been a great tower of strength to our denomination. He has made a contribution to our denomination as a state leader. He has lived a consistent and helpful life among us. When problems arose, we just instinctively turned to Dr. _____ for help.

Words of Thanks

Public

I would like to give a special word of appreciation to Mr. _____ for his efficient planning and tireless efforts to make this program an actuality. He undertook the task, knowing how many hours of time it would call for, but he did it without hesitation. We are most grateful for a job well done.

⚮

As we close, I would like to say a word of thanks to the one who brought us our program tonight. She has stated in crisp compactness the juicy spiritual truths she has found from diligent study. Ms. _____, we thank you for coming our way and giving us such a fine message.

⚮

We certainly are grateful for the program given tonight by Mr. _____. The pictures he has shown of his travels on our mission fields have made us feel more a part of the work. We cannot all have the opportunity to travel, but by listening to Mr. _____ and seeing his pictures, we feel more appreciation for the things he has told us about.

We wish to thank our guest this evening for a very enlightening message on art. We have a deeper appreciation of good paintings after this evening.

To be used at the close of an all-day meeting.

Appreciation

So early on this Fall morning
    You came from near and far,
To dear old First Church _____
    Who set her doors ajar.

Thank you for the fellowship,
    Thank you for the food and fun.
Thank you for the Christ-like spirit in
    The work that you have done.

And dear Mrs. _____'s message,
    How much it meant today;
She blessed each one who listened
    In a special sort of way.

Mrs. _____ has been our leader
    For just a few short years,
But as she now will leave us,
    The future has no fears.

She's been a faithful leader,
    She's trained us well and so
Let's pledge each one to pray for her
    Wherever she may go.

Thank you workers for your service
    Whether great or small,
May you be found faithful,
    Listening to God's call.

Thanks to you, _____, we have just spent a wonderful hour listening to your great message. You have inspired us to go forth and seek to attain higher goals in life.

I wish to pay a public tribute to one of our truly great women. As a minister's wife, she has given herself to God's work on earth. We wish to thank her for being one of us these past years. Often we neglect to tell her how grateful we are for her contributions to our church.

We wish to say thanks to one who saw a great need in our church and met that need with a generous gift.

We thank God for giving us people who will share their wealth in order to make our places of worship more comfortable and appealing.

I want to say a word of thanks to our missionaries, Mr. and Mrs. _____. They have meant a lot to this area. They have given our churches some help for which we will ever be grateful and thankful.

We wish to say thank you for the methods you have used, working through the churches. You have given us a feel and a vision of the work, and we thank God for you.

A special word of thanks goes to all those who stepped in at the last minute to assist in the program and banquet preparations. It would be impossible to call all by name; the entire occasion was an excellent example of cooperation by so many—young and old alike.

Personal

We do not realize how much friends mean until times of stress and anxiety. Thank you so much for coming to visit us at the hospital and encouraging us during a trying ordeal.

With deep gratitude I wish to thank you for _____. My heart overflows as I think of your unselfish gift. We will do our best to make this gift count for good in God's kingdom work. Eternity alone will reveal the good you have accomplished. We wish to express to you our sincere thanks.

ॐ

I wish to express my personal thanks to those who took my place while I was in the hospital. I had no way of knowing an emergency would arise when I started plans for the youth program. It sounds as if my dear substitutes were more than successful. Thanks again for carrying on while I was ill.

ॐ

Thank you for your graciousness in inviting us to spend a few days in your lovely home. We have enjoyed every minute of our visit and hope you will ask us to come again sometime.

ॐ

The fine art of a "Thank You," to friends,
  so they hear,
Bring a blessing to two every time;
Both the one with the tongue and the one with the
  ear
Are so blest that neglect is a crime.

—J.T. Bolding

ॐ

Each time I wear my beautiful birthday gift, my heart will be gladdened. Knowing such precious friends as you makes my life richer each day.

Thank you for the lovely gift and sweet card.

Friends like you are a part of my "daily bread." Your friendship means so much to me. Each time I see your generous and lovely gift I will think of you. Thanks so much for making my graduation day so happy.

In time of sorrow and grief there is so much comfort in the food you brought and the beautiful card you sent.

Thank you so much for the beautiful fall flowers. I am enjoying them very much. You were both kind and thoughtful to remember me.

You will never know just what you mean to me. I wish I could tell you what is in my heart. Since there are not enough words in the English language to fully express it, I will just say I appreciate you.

At this special time of the year, it is nice to be thought of. You have brought me all the joys of the season with this lovely gift. We wish for you a blessed and happy Christmas and many joys in the New Year.

The beautiful antique lamp you gave me will always remind me of my happy years spent in my grandmother's home as a child.

This gift will be a constant reminder of your dear friendship. I deeply treasure your love. Thank you.

Thank you for your kind hospitality. There is nothing I like better than visiting with dear friends like you.

For Thank-You Notes

Thank you for teaching in my place. You have a light touch that softens the truth you deliver, the truth we need to hear. You are a delight and a blessing to our church; we are so glad you came our way.

A Teacher's Thanks

Such a class I never knew
Filled with ladies just like you.
To make others happy
Seems to be your aim.
Since teaching you
Life for me can never be the same.
I love you, I love you
Oh please let me say,
And thank you so much
For a happy birthday.
The gift you gave is oh so pretty
I must close this silly little ditty.
If I should lose any of you
I'd say, "Oh, what a pity."

✍

You have such a great gift, which you have dedicated to the Lord's use. Thank you for your part in today's program.

✍

I would like to thank you for recommending me for the job at _____. You were kind to take a personal interest in me. As I enjoy this new position, I will ever be grateful for your help in securing the place.

✍

Our sorrow is easier to bear with the help of friends like you. We appreciate all you have done for us during our recent bereavement.

✍

Thank you for the gift you sent. The book was very stimulating. We shall read and cherish it for a long time.

✍

The wedding gift you sent was just the thing we needed. You were so kind to remember us on our happy day. Thank you very much for the useful gift.

✍

Thank you for your many visits during our recent bereavement. In times like we have just experienced, we realize more than ever how much friends mean to us. You will always hold a treasured spot in our hearts because you were so kind to us.

Thank you for your visit to our church. You were an inspiration to all who attended the services. Thank you for all your work and effort on our behalf. We covet a future visit from you to our church.

Thank you for speaking in our chapel. Your message was very timely and fitting. We will look forward to the time when you can be with us again.

To my way of thinking nothing will compare
With lots of good neighbors whose customs are rare.
They are the most considerate, day in and day out,
As good as real angels, without any doubt.
If you're sick or you're well, no difference it makes
They stand by you through all with whatever it takes.
They tell me in cities you don't know the name
Of folks you live right by—I think that's a shame.
I may be old fashioned, but just take it from me—
Among a lot of good neighbors is the best place to be.
I one time imagined that when I grew old
There'd be nothing like owning a lot of real gold.
My fancies have changed now, and I've learned by this
     time
It's not gold I'll enjoy most; but these neighbors of
     mine.

—Anonymous

✑

Thank you for being so sweet and kind. Your cards, letters, and gifts have been deeply appreciated during this trying time.

✑

Thank you for your visits and sympathy. My prayer is that we may work for one cause and really be laborers together with God.

✑

Thank you for your kind letter and for your kind words in regard to my small gift. You are one of the most beloved people in our church. We appreciate your stabilizing influence.

✑

Thank you so very much for your gift. Now that I am finally getting settled in my new home, I can hardly wait to start using it.

✑

Dear friend, we enjoyed so very much the good meal in your home. Man may live without money, man may live without books, but where are the men who can live without cooks? We truly did enjoy so very much the good food you prepared for us. More than that, we enjoyed getting to know your family better and having fellowship with them.

Thank you so much for the guiding hand you gave us in the starting of a new organization. The difficulties would have been so much greater without your experienced help. Thank you so much. Be sure to meet with us again when you have time.

Just a note to you as chairman of our entertainment committee. The food and decorations you prepared were so good and so pretty. Thank you for a job well done.

Words of Cheer

When the day is dark and gloomy
And the fog obscures your view,
And you feel there is no challenge
Waiting anywhere for you;
When it's routine you must follow
Through a dreary weather chart,
And you feel the hand of duty
Like a millstone on your heart;
Face the skies however darkened,
When you ache to turn away
Do the job that lies before you,
Keep your courage one more day.
You can never guess how often
You affect another's life
By the fact you are a doer
Not a quitter in the strife.

—Selected

If I thought that a smile of mine
   Might linger the whole day through
And lighten some heart with a heavier part,
   I'd not withhold it—
Would you?

If you would be cheerful and spread cheer around try this recipe:
   Be interested—don't try to be interesting.
   Be pleasing—don't expect to be pleased.
   Be entertaining—don't wait to be entertained.
   Be lovable—don't wait to be loved.
   Be helpful—don't ask to be helped.

Joke with him who jostles you,
Smile on him who hurries you,
Laugh at him who pushes you,
   It doesn't cost a cent!
Don't be carrying around that chip
Wink your eye and curve your lip,
And from life's sunshine take a sip,
   It doesn't cost a cent!
Don't be always first to rile
Your neighbor—give him just a smile,
It will cheer the dullest, while
   It doesn't cost a cent!

                 —Anonymous

✑

You have had a loss and a heartache. We are so sad for you. Try to keep in your heart all that was happy and worth keeping and with a breath of kindness blow the rest far away.

✑

If you wish to be cheerful and happy, we'll tell you the way: Don't live tomorrow till you've lived today.

✑

The happy, cheerful life is not made up of one huge ray of sunshine. The sunshine of life is made up of many little beams which brighten our pathways.

✑

Today life seems to you to have lost its glow. There are many happy days yet before you. Think of the blessings you have left. Remember that even a tiny little dewdrop in the morning sun is big enough to reflect the sunshine. You have much for which to be thankful left.

For Notes of Cheer

We think of you so often. We wish for you a speedy recovery and the best of health. May the good Lord always keep you in his care. Thank you for your nice letter.

∽

Each day warm thoughts of you fill our hearts. We hope good wishes and happiness will soon be your portion each day. Your note was appreciated.

∽

You are such a nice friend to remember. We think of you during this trying time. We pray that God will soon restore you to health and happiness. Many thoughts and prayers are offered for you at this time.

∽

Here's wishing today is a happy day for you. We remember you very warmly. Your thoughtful little note was greatly appreciated.

∽

Especially today we are thinking of you. We have only good wishes for you in this new venture. We will not cease to pray that God will give you success and happiness. You are missed in our circle of friends.

∽

Cheery greetings to one we all love. Just thought I would send a note to say we are wishing you sunny hours always, with much, much happiness all your days.

∽

Hi! Just a note of friendly cheer. I'd like to say "Hello." You are such a nice friend; I wish we could be closer together and visit to and fro. Come any time you can.

ဢ

"Hello, and how are you?" I feel inclined to say, to hope you are having a happy day. I wish for you all the pleasant things which make life sweet and good.

ဢ

Every day of the year I'm wishing for you the best of happiness and good cheer. We think of you often with thoughts of love and pray God's blessings be showered on you from above.

ဢ

May all your wishes come true, today, tomorrow, and always. We sincerely wish the very best for you and yours. We think of you with warm, happy thoughts.

ဢ

Just a note to let you know I'm thinking of you. Never a day goes all the way through but I am thinking sometime of you. I cherish your friendship.

ဢ

Just wishing you were here! We miss your pleasant ways, your happy smile, your words of cheer. Every day we wonder when you will come our way again.

ဢ

It is so nice to think about someone like you. You're in my thoughts often, and I hope for your happiness always. We miss your warm and friendly touch. At our house you're liked so very, very much.

❦

A friendly little note to say it's true, we think so very much of you. You're in my thoughts as I write today and wish you were not so far away.

❦

I just got to thinking about you on this pretty spring day. You are a dear friend in a special sort of way. So, hello and best wishes; we love you very much.

❦

So sorry to hear you have been ill. May heaven send good health to you soon. Best wishes for happy days just ahead of you. Always remember, someone thinks of you and prays each day that the very best health will come your way.

❦

I hope you feel better. I know that you should if all the wishes I'm making are doing any good.

❦

We are so glad to know you are out of bed for part of each day. Here's hoping you are soon so much better you can stay up all day. We have missed you very much in our services. Your presence is always an inspiration to me. Best wishes for a speedy recovery.

❦

May each hour of your day be blessed with cheer. May blue skies shine again over you. We wish for you com-

fort, hope, and courage. We long to see again that twin-
kle in your eye. So here's hoping the clouds of illness
soon pass you by.

May better health bring cheer to you today and all this
week through. May friendly friends bring cheer and fun
as they call on you one by one. We love you and miss
you and will be so glad when you are again with us.

Dear friend, you are having some troubles just now.
May your faith so deep and true help at this time to guide
you through. I know that God in countless ways will
soon grant you brighter, happier days.

God sends the sunshine and God sends the rain. Our
world must have both from time to time. I am sorry it is
a cloudy time for you, but we are praying God will
brighten the view and sunshiny days will soon come for
you.

Words
of Congratulation

On Birthday Anniversary

I'm sending a wish most warm and true because it is meant just for you. On your special day my very best wishes are sent your way. Please have a very happy day. May God's richest blessings be showered upon you.

As days ahead unfold, may life's richest blessings be yours, not just on your birthdays but all the days of life. Congratulations on your birthday and be assured of our love and regard always.

May God's great love be with you on this your birthday. It is such a pleasure to know you and I wish for you blessings always every day.

How great is God's goodness to let us live from year to year. May you have a blessed birthday filled with rich blessings of love. I pray the coming year will for you be filled with cheer and the sunshine of God's love.

So today is a milestone along life's way. May God grant you happiness; may your cherished dreams and hopes come true. We love you and will pray for you all the year through.

In many different ways I wish you all God's blessings. I hope your birthday and all the days ahead will be pleasant. With God's truth to guide you in everything you do, how can your best wishes fail to come true?

May God keep you in his constant tender care, this is for you my birthday prayer. May each year grow sweeter and life seem more sweet.

Congratulations on your birthday. May God bless your heart and life. May your days be filled with every happiness. May all your wishes great or small come true to make this your happiest birthday of all.

Happy Birthday! May God really bless you all through the coming year. May all your days be useful and happy.

Birthday greetings, and may I say, we hope God blesses you with health and happiness. We hope joy grows in your heart each day of the coming year. May all the future too be filled with dreams that will come true.

On Wedding Anniversary

It's time for happy greetings because your anniversary is here. So nice you have been married for many happy years. Now what could be more fitting than for me to say we hope you have a very special, happy day. May God's richest gifts forever come your way.

Happy anniversary! Just a friendly little note to wish happiness to a couple I like so very much. May God grant you many more happy years together.

We are thinking of you on your wedding anniversary. We send best wishes to say we love you. May the years to follow be sweeter than those just past. May your home be a place where happiness reigns.

‱

I'm hoping that this little note will show at least a part of all the happiness I wish you deep down inside my heart. The pleasant things you do and say brighten up so many dreary days. Since this is your special anniversary, I hope you have a very pleasant time.

‱

Congratulations on your anniversary. I count it a joy just to be friends with a couple I admire so much. I wish I could show the friendly thoughts I have for you.

‱

To me you are special. You are never out of my mind. You are both so friendly and always more than kind. So please let me say, "Best Wishes, Best Wishes, on your Anniversary."

‱

Happy Anniversary! May sunshine fill your home today. May God's blessings gladden your hearts and strengthen you for life's trials. It has been such a joy to know you these many years. Congratulations on your rearing such a fine family. God has indeed been with you and blessed you. May he continue to do so is our prayer today.

‱

There is surely no time as good as the present to say congratulations and blessings to you. May God always bless you your whole lives through.

On this very special day we wish for you everything pleasant and happy.

Congratulations extra warm and true, because this is a very happy day for you. I wish this little note could show just how much we long for you to know happy days and prosperous ones too.

Happy Anniversary to both of you. We recall fond memories of years gone by. We wish for you much happiness in the years ahead. To us you are a very special pair.

On the Birth of a Child

Congratulations to the parents of a baby so new and sweet. May everlasting joy be yours and grow deeper each year.

"Jesus . . . took them up in his arms, . . . and blessed them" (Mark 10:16).

Congratulations to you in this blessed event. May God bless you as you care for this little bundle of love. It is a pleasure to know such a nice couple as you has been blessed with a sweet, healthy baby.

"Happy shalt thou be, and it shall be well with thee" (Psalm 128:2).

So now you are a brand-new mom and dad! May your sweet little guest bring you joys untold. God has trusted this little one to you and may you have the blessings parenthood brings. We are so proud of you.

We are so happy that a baby dear and sweet has come to live at your house and make your lives complete. We know he will have the best of care because he has chosen such sweet parents, so there—congratulations!

God bless you as you enjoy and care for your new baby. I am reminded of a little verse I read someplace.

> There are clocks to tell the time of day,
>   And scales to tell the weight of hay;
> But what rule, sir, would you employ
>   To tell the worth of a girl or boy?
> Measures there are for silver and gold,
>   By carats the worth of diamonds are told;
> But there is no measure in all the earth
>   To tell what a boy or girl is worth!

May your cup run over with happiness as you care for your new little darling.

So God has sent you a new little bundle of cheer! Good luck and God bless you as you stand in wonder and joy and hold your own precious baby. We will pray for you often as the problems arise and know you will be parents so good and so wise.

Congratulations on your new baby! You will find parenthood to be a blessing and a delight. Blessings carry responsibilities, but you are both such fine Christians, I know your little one will be brought up in the very best Christian way. The little one is to be congratulated upon having such wonderful parents as I know you will be.

Dear friends, we are so glad God opened up heaven and sent a little bit of sunshine to dwell in your home. We wish for you every happiness as you rear this little child. May God bless and keep her safe.

On Graduation

May we take this opportunity to extend personal regards to you on the occasion of your graduation from high school. We hope you will go on to college and find great happiness and success in life.

My best wishes for many years of success as you go forth to meet the world a college graduate. You have studied long and hard. We are very proud of the record you have made. May life bring to you much happiness and contentment.

Congratulations to you. You deserve the very best life has to offer. Now you have achieved the coveted diploma. The world offers you a challenge; may you also offer the world a challenge as you go forth to establish yourself in your chosen career. Always be assured we will be praying for life to give you the best, for you to live up to the standards your home and church have taught you.

Best wishes and congratulations for four years of work well done. Our whole town is proud to call you a native son. As you are about to launch out to make your way in the world, I would remind you,

> Only one life,
> 'Twill soon be past,
> Only what's done for Christ
> Will last.

Never forget to live as you have been taught, with the highest goals before you.

Congratulations! We are very proud you are now a college graduate. Through the years we have watched with pride as you grew up. We have always been glad when you succeeded in some project. Now you are about to face the greatest project of all: life on your own. If you will indulge an old friend, I would like to give you a bit of advice.

If you want to be rich. . . . GIVE!
   If you want to be poor. . . . GRASP!
      If you want to be needy. . . . HOARD!
         If you want abundance. . . . SCATTER!

—Selected

❧

Congratulations on your graduation! We are so glad to welcome you back to your hometown. We know you will take your place as a leader among us. Call on us to help in any way we can as you are getting adjusted to a new type of life. We especially look forward to having you in our church.

❧

Best wishes! Today is a great day in your life. We hope it is a day of joy as you close the page on your school days and open the door for new beginnings as a part of the everyday world.

❧

Best wishes to you. We are proud of you. May God bless and keep you as you make crucial decisions concerning work and places to live during the days just ahead. Rest assured that our prayers and thoughts are with you.

On a Special Achievement

Dear friend, let me congratulate you on the award you received at the Music Festival last week. My heart swelled with pride as I read the account in the local paper. It makes me so happy that one so talented uses that talent to help the music program of our church.

It gives me real joy to be able to write and say how very pleased we were you won the memory verse contest. If more boys and girls worked at memorizing the way you have, our school would be quite outstanding. You have been an inspiration to all of us.

We would like to congratulate the youth department on the wonderful program they gave before our church last week. All who were present received a blessing. Our church is fortunate indeed to have such dedicated young people.

May I express gratitude and congratulations to all who worked so hard and faithfully to make our church dinner a success. We were very proud of the offering given, of the program, and especially of the spirit of goodwill which prevailed. Thanks for a job well done.

May I take this opportunity to express appreciation to the teachers and officers who have worked so faithfully during the past year. Your work has been quite outstanding. Our church has grown in membership and in spirit.

Many thanks to the many who made possible the wonderful report given at our last business meeting. It is a great joy to work with people who are such marvelous Christians.

Congratulations to Mr. _____ and his committee on the successful way they handled the "Back to Church Day" last Sunday. Their faithful work is very much appreciated. May God bless them, each and every one.

Congratulations to Ms. _____, one of our faithful members, on her being elected to the position of school principal at our local high school. Our church is proud to see one we know to be a fine Christian receive this promotion.

Congratulations! We have just heard about your being selected to receive a scholarship to _____ college. You are a very deserving young person and it gives us joy to know you will have this scholarship to help you enter a new phase of life.

At Christmastime

There is a time for jingling bells,
Holiday laughter and children's yells,
For hurry and scurry, toys warm and furry. . . .
Bright lights on the tree. . . .
Wishes warm as wishes can be,
Merry Christmas.

Remember, as we celebrate his birth,
That we have a duty on this earth,
With trust in him and with a spirit of love,
We must renew our faith and dedicate our efforts
To accomplish the ideal of Peace on Earth.

What is Christmas? Is it a tranquil snowy scene, brightly wrapped gifts, a time of rejoicing over new possessions? Christmas is a time to be filled with love, good cheer, and satisfactions of friends heard from after a long time. Christmas is a time to worship in an "old fashioned" way.

ᴄᴏ

Christmas, in case we forget it, commemorates the birth of Christ. It is a day to rejoice over the greatest gift of all, our Savior. "Glory to God in the highest, and on earth, peace, goodwill toward men."

ᴄᴏ

The colorful symbols, bright, sparkling, bring forth silent thoughts of the expressions of true joy and delight found at the Christmas season. Everyone on our staff wishes to express to you our thanks and appreciation for your cooperation during the past year. Our purpose for the coming year is to merit your continued faith and love.

These are our Christmas wishes to you and yours.

ᴄᴏ

May we take this opportunity to thank you one and all for your beautiful greetings and gifts. We extend to you our warmest wishes. Happy holiday!

ᴄᴏ

Bells ring out merrily for all our loyal friends. We wish you the same generous measure of happiness you have given us this past year.

ᴄᴏ

Christmastime affords us the opportunity to express our heartfelt gratitude for the friendship and love you have shown us during the year.

Let's make a joyful noise this Christmas. Let's deviate from thoughts of holiday food and beautiful presents. Let us think most about CHRISTmas. Do something to promote CHRISTmas in the hearts around you.

Sincere Christmas Greetings come from all of us to each of you as we approach this significant season. Let me assure you of our prayerful interest in you at this holiday season. We trust that this will be your most joyous Christmas, and that the New Year will hold for you God's choice blessings.

At this season pray for us; we shall for you.

A verse printed in the *Dallas Morning* news in the year 1909 or 1910.

At Christmas

We're getting awfully good at home
  You ought to come and see
Why Sis, she's changed so much these days
  She's even nice to me.
And I'm as good as custard pie
  Always saying please.
Have to walk a tight rope you know
  Christmas times like these.

But Paw he has an awful grouch.
   When he comes home at night
Maw puts his slippers by the fire
   And Sis hands him a light.
And I just run my fool legs off
   A'doing silly stunts
But Paw he never says a word
   Just looks at us and grunts.

If I had money like he's got
   I'd smile to us and say
Here's twenty dollars, folks
   Go spend it right away!
Christmas comes but once a year
   And Paw he's awful mean
For Christmas time is almost here
   Just a week between.

                —Harry Lee Mariner

    One of the joys of the holiday season is the opportunity to put aside the routine of everyday affairs. We like to send best wishes to all our friends and wish for them a happy and prosperous New Year.

It is Christmas in the mansion,
   Yule-log fires and silken frocks;
It is Christmas in the cottage,
   Mother's filling little socks.
It is Christmas on the highway;
   In the thronging, busy mart;

> But the only lasting Christmas
> Is when Christ is in the heart.
>   —Selected

꧁

Try this recipe if you would have a Merry Christmas:
Take the crisp cold of a December night, add two generous parts of snow, stir in air so clear it tinkles. Into a generous heart mix the wonder of a little girl, the sparkle of a young boy's glance, the love of parents, and set gently before the chimneyside. Add the lightest touch of the reindeer's hooves, a sprig of holly, a scent of fir. Set the mixture to rise in the warmth of a dream of goodwill to men. It will be almost ready to serve when it bubbles with warmth and good feeling. Bedeck with the light of a star set in the East, garnish with shining balls of gold, silver, and red. Serve to the tune of an ancient carol in the middle of the family table. This recipe is sufficient for all men and women you will ever meet.

—Anonymous

꧁

> 'Tis Daybreak in the hearts of men,
>   for Christmastide
> Fills all the waiting world
>   With music!
>   —Christmas Plaque

༄

Then pealed the bells more loud and deep:
"God is not dead, nor doth he sleep;
The wrong shall fail, the right prevail,
With peace on earth, good will to men."

       —Henry Wadsworth Longfellow

༄

A gleam of love-light in the eye;
   A glint of gladness in the sky;
An added charm in passers-by—
   That's Christmas!

A hint of halo in the day;
   A thought of "others" when we pray;
A gentle glow that lights the way—
   That's Christmas!

A goodwill flame within the heart;
   A zeal to act a nobler part;
An urge the upward way to start—
   That's Christmas!

       —E. C. Baird

༄

One must be poor to know the luxury of giving.

༄

As we enter the Christmas season, let us pray for hope,
that there will soon be peace in our world. For love in

our hearts for those less fortunate than ourselves. For perservance to seek a better understanding of those with whom we come in contact each day. For courage to face trouble and trials bravely. For optimism that our world will become a better place. For the ability to bring joy to others, which is the true spirit of Christmas.

Since God gave us the wonderful gift of his son, there has grown up different traditions and customs concerning Christmas gifts.

In Germany, the people say they receive their gifts from Kriss Kringle, a young girl wearing a golden crown and carrying a small Christmas tree.

In Denmark, gifts will come from an elf, Jule-nissen. Throughout the year, the elf lives in the attic of the home to keep an eye on the household. On Christmas Eve, a bowl of rice and milk is served in the attic home before the family eats.

Gifts come from the stars in Poland, from the angels in Hungary, and in Syria children wait for the Gentle Camel.

In Russia, the bearer of gifts is an old woman named Baboushka. She is supposed to take gifts to all the children as she searches for the Christ child.

In America we look for gifts from dear old Santa Claus.

It is fun for small children to look for different myths at Christmastime, but as Christians we must try to teach them the true meaning of Christmas and always keep before them the story of the greatest giver and the greatest gift, Christ Jesus.

Our Gifts to Him

Gifts of the Wise Men brought Him of old:
    Frankincense fragrant, myrrh and pure gold.
Gift of the teacher brought Him today:
    Ideals for pupils, lighting their way.

Brought by the surgeon: Limbs straight and strong,
    From those which had been twisted so long.
Engineer: bridges; mason: great walls;
    Railroader: schedules; postman: sure calls;

Ranchman: his cattle; farmer: his crop;
    Salesman: his orders; merchant: his shop;
Father: provisions, example and care;
    Mother: caresses, devotion and prayer.

Each with the talent grace has bestowed,
    Used for God's glory in earth's abode.
And the Lord treasures that which we give;
    Blesses our effort, helps us to live.

Gifts of the Wise Men? Yea, let them meet
    Gifts from us always at Jesus' feet.

—J.T. Bolding

As we celebrate his birth, let us remember that our duty to mankind is growing greater in this great world. With a spirit of love, help us to renew our faith and dedicate our efforts to bring to the world our Christ of peace and understanding.

Christmas is the season of good wishes and goodwill, a season for families, for memories, for sacrifice, and for gifts to those we love. If we want Christmas to truly come, we must let Christ dwell in our hearts and guide our actions.

Bits of Humor

Oh, I could thank the Lord a lot,
    For all the things I haven't got.
For measles, mumps and pigeon toes,
    Knobby knees and drippy nose,
A disposition sticky sweet,
    Grasping kinfolks, great big feet.
There's lots I could be glad of too,
    But I'm just thankful I have you!

Now you've got me, for a speech.

                —Anonymous

    Have you ever heard of people who get all their exercise jumping to conclusions? Don't conclude I am not going to speak. I have it on the tip of my tongue. Sometimes my tongue just gets tied in knots. Then I can't find the tip to get started on the things I have to say.

Some speeches I have heard remind me of a turkey with his tail feathers spread. He makes an elegant impression but the feathers don't represent much meat.

I hope I am not like some speakers. They can't broaden or deepen their messages, so they lengthen them.

Two kinds of people seem determined not to get what they pay for: the church members and the students.

The three hardest things to do: climb a ladder leaning toward you, kiss a girl leaning away from you, and *deliver a commencement address* (adapt this to suit the occasion).

Well, I have tried to climb a ladder leaning toward me, I've delivered a commencement address before, and I— well, let's start our work together.

A small child prowling in her grandmother's purse looked innocently up and said, "Have you coughed up all your cough drops?"

People love a dog because he wags his tail and not his tongue.

∽

The upper crust is often a bunch of crumbs held together by a wad of dough.

∽

It has been suggested that we have a new issue of a postage stamp bearing a picture of the weeping taxpayer.

∽

Hay fever can be either positive or negative. Sometimes the eyes have it and sometimes the nose.

∽

Some say it is more blessed to give than to receive, but most of us get the most fun out of being on the receiving end.

∽

Truth is always the object of philosophy, but not always the object of philosophers.

—John Collins

∽

Ten Fold Greatness of a Man

He came into a great heritage.
He brought to his task a great qualification.
He embraced and energized a great program.
He built a great organization.
He ministered to a great constituency.

He promoted a great unity.
He conducted a great business.
He achieved great results.
He exerted a great influence.
He transmitted a great trust.

—Hight C. Moore

Benevolence

Though I speak of missions with the tongue of eloquence and have not love,

I am become as sounding brass, or a tinkling cymbal.

And though I have the gift of prophecy, and understand all Bible study and though I have all faith so that I could be president of our organization, and have not love, I am nothing.

And though I give from my pantry to the poor in my community, and though I burn with zeal for civic reforms and have not love it profiteth me nothing.

And now abideth faith, hope, love, these three; but the greatest of these is love.

—Selected

Opportunity—oh the glory of it! . . . "To make known to the sons of men his mighty acts and the glory of the majesty of his kingdom" (Psalm 145:12).

All plans of stewardship will fail us
Unless Jesus guides all the way:

His spirit will bless and give us success
    If we will WORK, and STUDY and PRAY.

              —Selected

∽

Where can a man buy a cap for his knee,
    Or a key to the lock of his hair?
Can his eyes be called an academy
    Because there are pupils there?

In the crown of his head what gems can be found?
    Who travels the bridge of his nose?
Can he use, when shingling the roof of his house,
    The nails on the end of his toes?

Can the crook of his elbow be sent to jail?
    If so, what did he do?
How does he sharpen his shoulder blades?
    I'll be hanged if I know, do you?

Can he sit in the shade of the palm of his hand?
    Or beat on the drum of his ear?
Does the calf of his leg eat the corn on his toes?
    If so, why not grow corn on the ear?

              —Anonymous

∽

If a man had half his wishes he would double his troubles.

              —Benjamin Franklin

The scissors grinder was talking happily to a friend. "This has been my biggest year. I have never seen things so dull."

When Pa Is Sick

When Pa is sick he's scared to death
An' Ma and us just hold our breath;
He crawls into bed an' puffs an' grunts,
An' does all kinds of crazy stunts.

He wants the doctor an' mighty quick,
For when Pa's ill he's awful sick.
An' sort o' sighs an' gasps an' groans;
He talks so queer an' rolls his eyes.

Ma jumps and runs an' all of us,
An' all the house, an' peace and joy
Is mighty skeerce—when Pa is sick.
It's somethin' fierce.

When Ma Is Sick

When Ma is sick she pegs away;
She's quiet though—not much to say.
She goes right on a-doin' things,
An' sometimes laughs, er' even sings.

She says she don't feel extra well,
But then it's just a kind o' spell.
She'll be all right tomorrow sure;
A good old sleep will be the cure.

An' Pa he sniffs an' makes no kick
For women folks is always sick.
An' Ma she smiles—let's on she's glad.
When Ma's sick, it ain't so bad.

—Selected

Satisfied

I read
In a book
That a man called
Christ
Went about doing good.
It is very disconcerting
To me
That I am so easily
Satisified
With just
Going about.

—attributed to
George Small

Young at Heart

How do I know my youth has been spent,
    Because my get-up-and-go, got up and went.
But in spite of all that, I'm able to grin
    When I think where my get-up-and-go has been.

Old age is golden, I've heard it said.
    But sometimes I wonder as I go to bed;

My ears in a drawer, my teeth in a cup,
   My eyes on a table until I wake up.

I get up each morning, dust off my wits,
   Pick up the paper and read the "obits."
If my name is missing, I know I'm not dead
   So I eat a good breakfast and go back to bed.

                          —Anonymous

A teacher was once trying to make an impression on his pupils.

"Now, pupils, if the solar declension is half past two in the afternoon, and equal to the living conditions in China, and the rate of travel includes the high cost of living in Pennsylvania, how old am I? Get out your calculator and figure that."

A bright pupil help up his hand: "You're thirty-six."

New teacher: "Right! How did you get the answer so quickly?"

"Well," the pupil replied, "My brother is only eighteen, and he is only half nuts."

A young man who had worked hard to graduate from college rushed out after graduation and shouted, "Here I am world; I have an A.B."

The world replied: "Sit down son, and I'll teach you the rest of the alphabet."

∽

After the love bug bites a young man, he soon has to start scratching for two!

∽

He talked of cabbage and kings. . . .
  Much was absurd;
And yet he had one saving grace:
  He could be heard.

—Spencer Leeming

∽

Is your problem child just a chip off the old block?

∽

The world that we're a-livin' in
  Is mighty hard to beat;
You get a thorn with every rose,
  But ain't the roses sweet!

—Anonymous

∽

A studious man was reading a book. He read that the world had had sixteen great rulers. He went lovingly up to his wife to tell her about it.

"Wife, do you know how many great rulers the world has had?" he asked.

"No," she replied. "But there is one less than you think there is."

A nice thing for a man to have up his sleeve is a funny bone.

Laugh a little now and then
   It brightens life a lot;
You can see the brighter side
   Just as well as not.
Don't go mournfully around,
   Gloomy and forlorn;
Try to make your fellow men
   Glad that you were born.
                    —Selected

She doesn't wink, she doesn't flirt
She spreads no gossip, tells no dirt.
She has no "line", she plays no tricks,
But give her time—she's only six.

A wealthy man once attended a missionary service. When the special offering was taken he gave a five cent piece. On the way home a storm came up and his car was turned over. He was trapped inside. Thinking of all the mean things he had done as he lay trapped and about to be crushed to death, he thought about the five cent piece he had just given to the poor missionaries. As he thought of this he became so small he easily crawled out from under the car.

The stingiest man in town was visiting with a neighbor on Sunday morning, in order to see the church services on television. All at once he jumped up and started to leave.

"What is wrong?" his friend asked.

"They are about to take the collection," he replied.

There is a feller that I know,
  Born just about so long ago
As I, and with me bound to grow—
  The boy inside o' me.

Sometimes I wish he were not there,
For when in games I'm not quite fair
He says to me, "Stop! Is that square?"
  The boy inside o' me.

It really does no good to hide.
A thing from him, b'cause I've tried.
And so I'm glad I'm on his side—
  That boy inside o' me.

—Author unknown

I eat my peas with honey
  I've done it all my life.
It makes the peas taste funny,
  But they will stay on my knife.

When we persist in using old-fashioned methods of promoting our work, we are just about like the fellow who penned this little rhyme.

Our visitor tonight has only been married for a short time. He had a hard time making some of his family and friends see the need for his marriage. "It is only puppy love," they told him.

As he went to the wedding, he told them, "It may be puppy love, but it is real to the puppy."

Apt Sentences

Meet success like a gentleman and disaster like a man.

You do not deserve happiness unless you give happiness to others.

> Servants of God, well done,
> Cease from thy loved employ—
> The battle's fought, the guerdon's won;
> Enter thy master's joy.

Gone are the days when we could postpone the important task until tomorrow, for we have learned it must be done today or never.

Engineers build plants on a low level, but they look to the hills for the source of power.

∽

There is no option for doing God's work.

∽

A task without a vision is drudgery.

∽

Fears, not years, make us old.

∽

> This world is a grand place to live in
> Cheery through and through,
> If everyone were just as kind as
> Folks like you.
>
> We won't reach all we aim for
> Every day, it's true;
> But one thing never fails us,
> Folks like you.
>
> I'm sure when we embark
> For shores beyond our view,
> We'll find that heaven's made of
> Folks like you.
>
> —Mrs. Francis N. Hays

∽

We have a world mission and can go far in the matter of changing the state of world conditions.

We must inspire our world with new hope and the realization of divine grace and the practicality of Christianity as the way out.

We celebrate today the growth of a denomination whose history is both romantic and sacred.

We are happy to report the most glorious record during the past year in the history of our church.

The past year has been filled with opportunities and victories, in spite of obstacles which pastors and workers have had to overcome.

The challenge is thrilling. Much has been done, but much more remains untouched, and every possible resource must be utilized to accomplish our task.

Some people keep talking, hoping they will think of something to say.

The motto of some speakers seems to be: "When you haven't prepared a message, filibuster."

∽

If you are content with the best you have done, you will never do the best you can do.

∽

He does the most in God's great world, who does the most in his own little world.

∽

God hath brought me to this hour.
                    —Abraham Lincoln

∽

If you would do better tomorrow, you must start doing better today.

∽

Life is a magic vase filled to the brim; so made that you cannot dip into it or draw from it; but it overflows into the hand that drops treasures into it—drop in malice and it overflows hate; drop in charity and it overflows love.

                                              —Ruskin

∽

The greatest use of a life is to spend it for something that outlasts it.

                                              —William James

◈

Castles in the air are all right until we try to move into them.

◈

Happiness can neither be prescribed by physicians nor dispensed by druggists.

◈

I am sorry for the man who can't feel the whip when it is laid on the other man's back.

—Abraham Lincoln

◈

We are marching to a cadence—
We have heard our Savior's voice
We will make His will and calling
To be life's work and choice.

◈

The roll of right beginnings is difficult to exaggerate.

—Roy McClain

◈

For work to be the most effective, you must be happy in the doing.

◈

All people smile in the same language.

Money isn't everything, but it's the best substitute there is for credit.

Keep your fears to yourself. Share your courage with others.

Some cause happiness wherever they go, others whenever they go.

Men sometimes credit themselves with their successes and God with their failures.

The greatest tragedy in life is not to fall down—it is to stay down.

Difficulties have a way of disappearing when people laugh at them.

Keeping the aquarium is not the same as fishing for men.

Do not let your life be mastered by the quest for things.

❦

Happiness is a sweet spring flowing from your devotion to God.

❦

To forget what is behind, you must look steadily ahead.

—Mark Allison

❦

Use it or lose it; that is the law of life in the spiritual as well as natural world.

❦

Gratitude is a fair blossom springing from the heart.

❦

To see what is right and not to do it, is to want of courage.

—Confucius

❦

The noblest motive is the public good.

—Virgil

∽

Love and skill working together can produce a masterpiece.

—Ruskin

∽

If you want to be loved, you must be lovable.

∽

He serves his party best who serves his country best.

—Rutherford Hayes

∽

Only one life t'will soon be past; only what's done for Christ will last.

∽

Leave town in such a way they will think you are leading the parade.

∽

Place yourself in a position where God can use you and he will wear you out.

∽

What did I do today that a person who is not a Christian could not have done?